Withdrawn

North Suburban Library District
ROSCOE BRANCH

All injuries to books beyond reasonable wear and all losses shall be made good to the satisfaction of the Librarian.

Each borrower is held responsible for all books drawn on his card and for all fines accruing on the same.

PLEASE NOTIFY US IF YOUR LIBRARY CARD IS LOST OR STOLEN

Been There!
INDIA

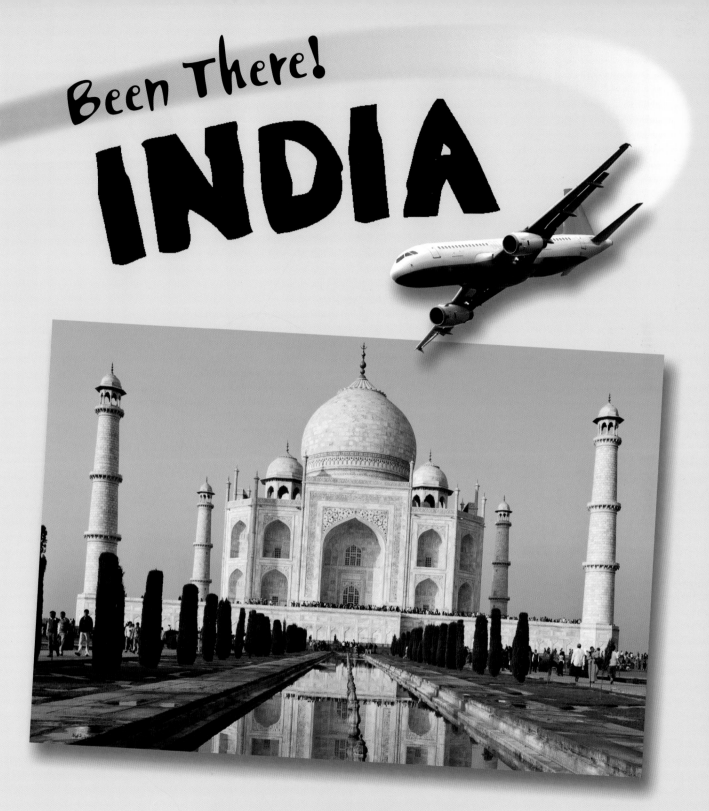

by Annabel Savery

A⁺

Smart Apple Media

Facts about India

Population: 1 billion

Capital City: New Delhi

Currency: Rupee (Rs)

Main Languages: Hindi and English

Rivers: Ganges, Brahamputra, Indus, Yamuna

Area: 1,269,345 square miles (3,287,590 sq km)

Published by Smart Apple Media
P.O. Box 3263, Mankato, Minnesota 56002

Printed in the United States of America at Corporate Graphics, in North Mankato, Minnesota.

Library of Congress Cataloging-in-Publication Data
Savery, Annabel.
 India / by Annabel Savery.
   p. cm. -- (Been there!)
 Summary: "Introduces India's major cities and landmarks, such as the Taj Mahal, the Golden Temple,
 and the Ganges River. Presents the daily activities and ceremonies of the Indian culture. Includes map
 diagrams and lessons on learning to speak and count in Hindi"--Provided by publisher.
 Includes bibliographical references and index.
 ISBN 978-1-59920-472-7 (library binding)
 1. India--Juvenile literature. 2. India--Description and travel--Juvenile literature. 3. India--History, Local--Juvenile literature. 4.
India--Social life and customs--Juvenile literature. I. Title.
 DS407.S265 2012
 954--dc22
          2010039595

Created by Appleseed Editions Ltd,
Planning and production by Discovery Books Limited
www.discoverybooks.net
Designed by Ian Winton
Edited by Annabel Savery
Map artwork by Stefan Chabluk
Picture research by Tom Humphrey

Picture credits: Corbis: p5 (Massimo Borchi), p8 main (John Hicks), p22 (Jon Hicks), p24 (Jon Hicks), p25 (Robert Wallis), p26
(Bob Krist) p27 (Robert van der Hilst); Discovery Picture Library: p6 (Chris Fairclough); FLPA: p23 (Vivek Sharma/Minden
Pictures); GettyImages: p8 bottom (Zubin Shroff), p9 top (jupiterimages), p10 (Walter Bibikow), p11 (Indranil Mukherjee), p16
(Christophe Archambault), p17 (The India Today Group); Istockphoto: p19 right (Indianeye); Photographers Direct: p9 bottom;
Shutterstock: title page & p13 (Holger Mette), p2 (R Gino Santa Maria), p7 (Pawel Pietraszewski), p10 inset (Paul Prescott),
p12 (Tian Zhan), p14 (Ajay Bhaskar), p15 (Paul Prescott), p19 left (Jeremy Richards), p20 (Regien Paassen), p21 (Nadina), p28
(Mikhail Nekrasov), p29 top (thefinalmiracle), p29 (Girish Menon); Wikimedia: p18 & p31 (Ken Wieland).

Cover photos: Istockphoto: main (shamanoo), right (indianeye); Shutterstock: left (tigerbarb).

DAD0046
3-2011

987654321

Contents

Off to India!

We are going on a vacation to India. It is a big country in the continent of Asia. The arrows on the map below show the places we will visit.

India is shaped like a diamond. The Himalayan Mountains are in the north. They are the highest in the world!

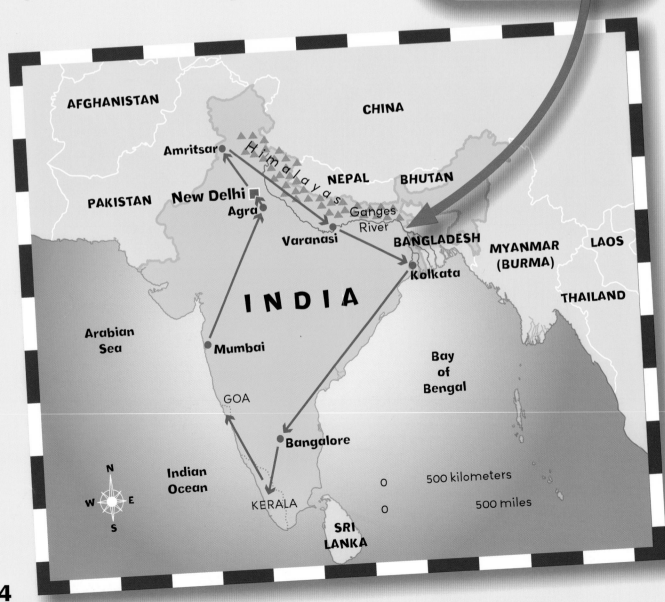

AFGHANISTAN

CHINA

Amritsar

Himalayas

NEPAL

BHUTAN

PAKISTAN

New Delhi

Agra

Ganges River

Varanasi

BANGLADESH

MYANMAR (BURMA)

LAOS

Kolkata

THAILAND

INDIA

Arabian Sea

Mumbai

Bay of Bengal

GOA

Bangalore

Indian Ocean

N W E S

KERALA

500 kilometers

500 miles

SRI LANKA

I am excited about visiting India. We are going in April when most of the country is hot, but it might still be cold in the north or high up in the hills.

Here are some things I know about India . . .

- The south of India is a peninsula. It is almost completely surrounded by water.
- Foods such as curry originally come from India, but they are now popular all over the world.
- Strong winds called "monsoons" bring heavy rain to India from June to September.

On our trip, I'm going to find out lots more!

Arriving in Mumbai

It is very hot when we get to Mumbai. We can feel the heat as soon as we get off the plane. Outside the airport, we get into a taxi, and Dad agrees on a price with the driver.

Lots of the taxis in the city look the same. They are black with yellow roofs. The streets are full of people. The drivers beep their horns and shout to each other.

As we drive through the city, we see big movie posters and lots of stalls and restaurants.

Some people are sitting on the sidewalk. They are selling food. Many people are shopping here.

Mumbai used to be called Bombay. The name was changed in 1996. Many people still call the city Bombay.

At the Beach

Mumbai is almost completely surrounded by sea. This means there are lots of beaches. We go to Chowpatty Beach.

Many people wear clothes like ours, but some of the women are wearing material wrapped around them. Mom says that this is a traditional Indian dress called a *sari*.

At the beach, we have a plate of tasty food called **bhelpuri.** There are lots of things in it, such as puffy rice, noodles, vegetables, and chili pepper.

Back at our hotel, a waiter tells us we should see a movie while we are here. He says that Mumbai is famous for its film industry, which is called "Bollywood."

Mumbai Station

From Mumbai, we are going to take a train to the city of Agra. The station building is very big and grand.

The roads to the station are full of vehicles, people, **rickshaws**, and even cows. Cows are **sacred** in India, so they are allowed to wander wherever they like.

Rickshaw

The station is busy. Everyone is trying to find the right train. I can see a big family with lots of bags. The parents, grandparents, and children are traveling together.

On the train, we have a sleeper compartment. There are bunks that fold down from the walls.

At each station we stop at, there are food vendors. We get off the train to buy snacks and stretch our legs.

Off to Agra

The journey to Agra is long. The city is in the state of Uttar Pradesh. The land here is good for growing crops because many rivers run through it.

On the way, we travel past the state of Rajasthan. The land here is different. In the east are mountains, and in the west there is the Thar Desert. People use camels to help them carry things across the desert.

In Agra, we go to see the Taj Mahal. It is a beautiful white building. Dad says that this is probably the most famous building in India and that lots of people visit here every year.

Did you know that the Taj Mahal took 22 years to build? The emperor Shah Jahan built it for his wife, Mumtaz Mahal.

Old Delhi, New Delhi

From Agra we travel north to New Delhi.

New Delhi is the capital city of India. The government of the country is based here.

The old parts of the city have been here for hundreds of years. The new parts have been built around them. The Lotus Temple is one of the modern-looking buildings.

We visit the Red Fort. It is a very big place with a long red wall around the outside. Dad says it is red because it is built using a type of red sandstone.

Every year on Independence Day, the **prime minister** of India makes a speech from here.

Independence Day is celebrated all over India on August 15. The British ruled India until 1947. Independence Day marks the day when the British government stopped ruling India and the Indian government took over.

Exploring New Delhi

One day we decide to buy our lunch from a street vendor.

He has many dishes. There are meat dishes, vegetable dishes, and thin, circle-shaped breads called **chapattis**. There are also dishes of chutney. Some of these are very spicy.

Then we go to the Akshardham Temple. This is a Hindu temple that is decorated all over with carvings of animals, figures, and patterns.

Many families are visiting the temple. Families in India are often large and usually live close together.

Did you know that about 80 percent of Indians are Hindus? There are many other religions in India, including Islam, Sikhism, Jainism, and Buddhism.

Out and About in Amritsar

The next stop on our trip is the city of Amritsar. It is a long way north in the state of Punjab.

In Amritsar, we visit the Golden Temple. The temple stands in the middle of a large pool of water. Its bright gold walls shine in the sun.

The Golden Temple is an important place for Sikhs. Many Sikhs live in the Punjab region. Sikh men wear **turbans**. This is a long piece of material wrapped around the head.

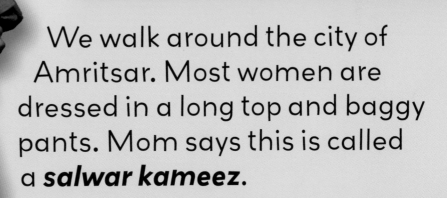

We walk around the city of Amritsar. Most women are dressed in a long top and baggy pants. Mom says this is called a *salwar kameez*.

Mom and I go into a clothing store. There are all sorts of brightly colored fabrics. The lady lets Mom try on a salwar kameez. It is very pretty.

The Ganges River

From Amritsar we are going to Varanasi. Many people come to Varanasi to bathe in the Ganges River, which flows through the city.

People use sets of steps called **ghats** to walk down to the river. They believe that bathing in the river washes away their sins. There are more than 80 ghats in the city.

Dad says that the Ganges River flows down from the Himalayas. It passes through many towns and villages. The river brings lots of water to this area. This makes it **fertile**. Crops grow well here.

A type of dolphin lives in the Ganges River. Ganges River dolphins are blind and find their food using echoes. Dad says that the dolphins are endangered, which means there are not many left.

The Old Capital

Our next stop is Kolkata. When the British ruled India, this was their capital. Later, they moved the capital city to New Delhi.

Kolkata is still a very important city. It is the biggest city in eastern India and the capital of the state of West Bengal.

In the evening, we go to see the Victoria memorial. This was built when the British ruled India. At night it is lit up in colored lights.

To the south of the city are the Sundarbans. This is a vast **mangrove** forest. A mangrove is a type of tree that grows in salty water.

The Sundarbans is an area filled with wildlife. There are many different types of birds. Monkeys and deer live here, too. There are also tigers!

Bustling Bangalore

After another long train ride, we arrive in the city of Bangalore. We have been on the train for three days.

There are lots of people rushing around the city. Dad tells me that many people work here. He says the city is growing very fast with lots of new businesses. Many people in Bangalore have good jobs and nice houses.

But there are poor parts of the city, too. Here people live in shelters made from sheets of metal or cardboard. Their lives are difficult because it is hard to get enough money to live and buy food.

Did you know that Bangalore was originally named after a dish of beans? Many stories tell of a king who liked a dish of beans so much that he named his fort after it.

Village Life

Next we are going to stay in a village in Kerala. This is a state in the southwest of India.

We travel to the village by bus. It is a long way, but it is a lovely trip through the countryside. It is very green in Kerala.

Most men in the village are farmers and work for a long time every day. The women help, too. These women (below) are carrying bags of tea they have harvested.

Going to School

The children from the families go to school a long way away. They have to walk 2 miles (3 km) to school every day. Some older boys have left the village. They have gone to look for work in the city.

Last Stop . . . Goa

The last place that we are going to visit in India is Goa. This is a small state on the west coast.

The first thing we do in Goa is go to the beach. It is beautiful and looks just like a postcard. The sea is blue and the sand is white. There are palm trees here, too.

Years ago, the Portuguese controlled Goa. Today, many Portuguese families still live here, and there are lots of old Portuguese buildings. Some people speak Portuguese, too.

Next, we go to a market. The vendors have all sorts of things for sale. There are beautiful clothes and sacks full of brightly colored spices.

Tomorrow we are going home, so we each buy a souvenir. These will remind us of our trip to India.

My First Words in Hindi

Lots of different languages are spoken in India. The main language is Hindi. Many people speak English, too. Here are some basic words in Hindi:

Namaste (*say* **Na-mas-tay)**   Hello

Krapayaa (*say* **Kree-pa-yaa)**   Please

Aap kiase hain?
(*say* **Aap kai-say hain)**   How are you?

Aapka naam kya hai?
(*say* **Aap-ka naam kyaa hai)**   What's your name?

Mera naam Susie hai.
(*say* **May-raa naam Susie hai)**   My name is Susie.

Counting 1 to 10

1 **ek**   (say **ehk**)   6 **chhe**   (say **cheh**)

2 **do**   (say **doo**)   7 **saat**   (say **saht**)

3 **tiin**   (say **teen**)   8 **aath**   (say **ahth**)

4 **chaar**   (say **chahr**)   9 **nau**   (say **naoo**)

5 **paanch**   (say **pahnch**)   10 **das**   (say **dahs**)

Words to Remember

bhelpuri a dish made from puffed rice, noodles, and chili pepper

chapattis round, flat bread

endangered threatened to become extinct, which means there will be no more of the species left in the world

fertile good for growing strong, healthy crops

ghats steps leading down to a river

mangrove a type of tree that grows in salty water

peninsula a piece of land that is almost completely surrounded by sea

prime minister the head of a government

rickshaw a small three-wheeled vehicle that can carry one or two passengers; a rickshaw is either pulled by a person on a bike, or has a small motor.

sacred shown great respect for religious reasons

salwar kameez an outfit of a long tunic top (kameez) and loose pants (salwar)

sari an outfit made from a light piece of material draped around the body

turban a headdress made from a long piece of material worn wrapped around the head

Index

Learning More about India

Books

A Day at an Indian Market (First Facts) Catherine Chambers, Capstone Press, 2011.

India (A World of Food) Anita Ganeri, Clara House Books, 2010.

India: The Land (The Lands, Peoples, and Cultures Series) Bobbie Kalman, Crabtree, 2010.

Web Sites

Geography for Kids, Geography Online, and Geography Games
http://www.kidsgeo.com/index.php

National Geographic Kids, People & Places
http://kids.nationalgeographic.com/kids/places/find/india

SuperKids Geography directory, lots of sites to help with geography learning.
http://www.super-kids.com/geography.html